GO Green
Shopping Choices

Helen Lanz

SEA-TO-SEA
Mankato Collingwood London

This edition first published in 2012 by

Sea-to-Sea Publications
Distributed by Black Rabbit Books
P.O. Box 3263, Mankato, Minnesota 56002

Printed in China

9 8 7 6 5 4 3 2

Published by arrangement with the Watts
Publishing Group Ltd, London.

Library of Congress Cataloging-in-Publication Data

Lanz, Helen.
 Shopping choices / by Helen Lanz.
     p. cm. -- (Go green)
 Includes index.
 ISBN 978-1-59771-304-7 (library binding)
 1. Shopping--Juvenile literature. 2. Shopping--Environmental aspects--
Juvenile literature. 3. Sustainable living--Juvenile literature. I. Title.
 TX335.5.L36 2012
 381'.1--dc22
                                    2011005509

Series Editor: Julia Bird
Design: D.R. ink
Artworks: Mike Phillips

Picture credits: G.M.B. Akash/Panos: 25; Antema/istockphoto: 15t; Noam
Armon/Shutterstock: 11c; Don Bayley/istockphoto: 7b; Ed Bock/Upper Cut
Images/Alamy: 27b; Kevin FitzMaurice-Brown/Alamy: 21b; Jaccek
Chabraszewski/istockphoto: 16; Deco/Alamy: 13t; Mikhail
Dudarev/Shutterstock: 14; Greg Balfour Evans/Alamy: 19b; Mars
Evis/Shutterstock: front cover b; Randy Faris/Corbis: front cover t;
Mike Flippo/Shutterstock: 10; © 1996 Forest Stewardship Council A.C.:18br;
Fotografica Basica/istockphoto: 20t; Angela Hampton/Alamy: 22t;
Cindy Miller Hopkins/Alamy: 6; Brian K/Shutterstock: 17b; Raphael Ramirez
Lee/Shutterstock: 7c; www.marmaxproducts.co.uk; Moodboard/Alamy: 12;
Keith Morris/Alamy: 18bl; Rex Morton/Photolibrary Wales/Alamy: 9t; Antonio
Jorge Nunes/Shutterstock: 24b; Edward Parker/Alamy: 8c; Alex Segre/Alamy:
21t; Ariel Skelley/Alamy: 26b; Daniel Stein/istockphoto: 14c;
Jack Sullivan/Alamy: 22b; Super Nova Images/Alamy: 15b;
Kevin Swope/Shutterstock: 26t: Urban Zone/Alamy: 20b;
Katherine Welles/Shutterstock: 8b.

To Kate—given the subject, this one's for you!

February 2011
RD/6000006415/001

"During 25 years of writing about the environment for the Guardian, I quickly realized that education was the first step to protecting the planet on which we all depend for survival. While the warning signs are everywhere that the Earth is heating up and the climate changing, many of us have been too preoccupied with living our lives to notice what is going on in our wider environment. It seems to me that it is children who need to know what is happening—they are often more observant of what is going on around them. We need to help them to grow up respecting and preserving the natural world on which their future depends. By teaching them about the importance of water, energy, and other key areas of life, we can be sure they will soon be influencing their parents' lifestyles, too. This is a series of books every child should read."

Paul Brown

Former environment correspondent for the UK's *Guardian* newspaper, environmental author, and fellow of Wolfson College, Cambridge, UK.

Contents

Words in **bold** can be found in the glossary on page 28.

Shop Till You Drop!

Have you been out shopping to spend your allowance lately? Maybe you've bought some new clothes? We all buy new things from time to time, and have to buy new clothes when we grow out of our old ones or they wear out.

Growing Demand

Our demand for new things grows every year. In the past, most people had less money, so they bought things only when they really needed them, and made them last. These days, we buy more things than people used to, and we keep them for less time before throwing them away. Importantly, there are also now many more of us than there used to be. The Earth's **population** has multiplied by four times in the last 100 years—and more people means more shoppers!

West Edmonton Mall in Canada is the biggest shopping center in North America. It has more than 800 retail outlets and is visited by more than 28 million shoppers a year.

6

What's the Cost?

Buying new things can be fun and exciting, but every step in the process of making new goods has a cost. This isn't just a money cost, but a cost to our **environment**. Making new goods uses up the Earth's **natural resources**. It also uses lots of **energy**, in the form of electricity, to process the goods, and in the form of fuel, to transport them all over the world. Finally, disposing of these goods takes its toll on the environment, too.

Container ships carry goods from country to country all over the world.

HOW MANY PAIRS?

In the United States, more than 450 million pairs of jeans are sold every year. That's 1.5 pairs of jeans for every person in the United States, including children.

In just one day, people from the U.S. buy 2,300,000 pairs of shoes. That's enough to cover about 11 football fields with shoe boxes!

The average American woman owns 27 pairs of shoes.

A World of Resources

Just think of all the things you use in one day! Everything that you wear and use has been made using the Earth's natural resources, including the invaluable resource, water.

From Factory to Living Room

Natural resources, such as wood, metal, and cotton, are gathered from forests, mines, and fields all over the world. They are taken to factories or plants where they are processed to make them into goods for us to buy. The goods are then transported from the factory to the stores where they will be sold.

Wood is being made into patio furniture at this factory.

Cotton grows in fluffy balls around the cotton plant's seeds.

What We Wear

Cotton is a type of fiber that comes from the seed pod of the cotton plant. We use it to make all sorts of clothes, from T-shirts to socks. To keep us warm, we wear sweaters, scarves, and hats made from wool, a thick fabric that comes from the coats of sheep. Our belts and shoes are usually made from leather, the dried and treated skin of animals.

Things We Use

It may not always be obvious, but the Earth's resources are also in everything we use. The glass you drink from has been made by heating sand and **minerals** at very high temperatures. The pencil you write with has been made from wood and a mineral called graphite. Even the plastic in your handheld computer game comes from the Earth (see case study).

 Plastic is produced in factories from natural materials.

I'm trying to make plastic but I must have gotten one of the ingredients wrong!

CASE STUDY

PREHISTORIC PLASTIC!

Plastic is a material made from oil, coal, natural gas, and salt. Oil, coal, and natural gas all developed under the ground from rotting plants and insects over millions of years. Because they have taken so long to form, they are called fossil fuels. A mixture of the ingredients is heated and processed to make plastic. So plastic, which can be light or heavy, hard or flexible, is actually made from prehistoric ingredients!

A Pricey Process

Are you wearing a T-shirt today? Many people are. Did you know that the T-shirt you're wearing could have traveled thousands of miles to reach you? It's probably traveled farther than you have in your whole life!

How to Make a T-shirt

Most T-shirts are made from cotton. Cotton is grown in fields, then **harvested** and transported to a factory where it is spun into thread and woven into sheets of fabric. It is then taken to another factory where it is cut to shape and stitched together to make T-shirts. The T-shirts are packaged and transported to shops where they are sold —often in a different country from where they have been made.

The cotton for these T-shirts was grown in India, but they were cut and stitched in China, and then transported to the U.S. where they are for sale.

A Pricey Process!

Every step in making a T-shirt costs money. We have to pay the farmer, factory workers, truck drivers or shippers, and retail assistants. It's also costly in terms of natural resources. Not only does our Earth provide us with the cotton to make the T-shirts with, it also provides the coal, oil, or gas to work the machines in the factories, and to fuel the trucks, ships, and planes that transport the clothes from factory to store.

Cotton is grown in countries such as the U.S., India, China, and Brazil, but may be transported thousands of miles before being sold.

COSTLY COTTON

It takes almost 1,500 gallons (5,625 l) of water—that's about 71 bathtubs-full—to make just 1.5 pounds (0.7 kg) of cotton.

About one-quarter of all the pesticides used in the world are sprayed onto cotton plants.

The machinery used to harvest cotton uses up about a pound (0.5 kg) of oil per pair of jeans.

All the Things in the World

It is a fairly simple process to make a T-shirt. If you think of all the things we can buy in our world, from houses and furniture to cars and computers, and what all these things are made from, then you can start to imagine how much of the Earth's resources we need to make, package, and transport them.

What a Waste!

Eventually, most of the things we buy are no longer needed. So what happens then? Well, depending on where we live and how we get rid of them, there are three main disposal methods. Waste can be buried in **landfill**, burned in **incinerators**, or **recycled**. Each of these processes has an impact on the environment.

A Lot of Rot

Most waste ends up in landfill. It takes a very long time for anything buried in a landfill to break down. In the meantime, despite being put in specially lined holes, as it rots, waste releases a smelly liquid called leachate. This can pollute our **groundwater** and soil. Rotting waste also gives off the **greenhouse gas** methane.

 A bulldozer on a landfill site.

How long it takes some natural and man-made objects to decompose.

OBJECT	TIME TO DECOMPOSE
Wool sock (natural)	1 year
Leather shoe (natural)	45 years
Disposable diaper (man-made)	About 550 years
Plastic jug (man-made)	Up to 1 million years

Did you know?

In the U.S., 3.5 tons of disposable diapers (about 18 billion) go into landfill each year! That's the same weight as two average-sized cars.

12

Up in Smoke

If things that we throw away aren't buried in landfill, they are often burned in giant incinerators. Burning garbage means that it does not take up valuable land space, unlike landfill. However, incinerators do give off several gases, including **carbon dioxide** (CO_2), which are harmful to our environment (see page 15).

Recycling

Recycling is the best way of getting rid of goods that we no longer want or use. When a product, such an old TV, is recycled, it is broken down into parts so that the **materials** from which it is made, such as glass and metal, can be used again. Recycling plants do use energy. Recycling's benefits however, are far greater than its drawbacks.

Electronic products ready for recycling.

CASE STUDY

NOT SO FANTASTIC PLASTIC!

Today, we make and use 20 times more plastic than 50 years ago, so that's 20 times more plastic to get rid of. The U.S. throws more than 17 million tons of plastic into landfill sites each year. That's like trying to bury nearly 3.5 million Indian elephants a year!

Can you imagine trying to bury 3.5 million elephants?

Getting Hotter

So you can see that what we buy doesn't just cost us the money we have to pay for the items. Everything we make and use has an effect on our environment. The use of fossil fuels in processing and transporting goods is also contributing to global **climate change**.

The Price of Production

Producing, or making, lots of new things uses up a lot of natural resources and fuel. The fuels used to power factories and plants are usually the fossil fuels of coal, oil, and natural gas. In the UK, more than 1.8 billion gallons (6.8 billion l) of oil are used to make clothing every year—enough to fill more than 2,700 Olympic-sized swimming pools.

Transportation

As we've seen, goods are often sold a long way from where they have been made. Trucks, ships, and planes are used to transport them around the world. Most transportation uses gasoline, a form of oil, which gives off fumes that pollute the air and contribute to climate change.

Power plants such as this one change fossil fuels into electricity.

Exhaust fumes from cars and trucks have helped form this layer of smog over Los Angeles.

Living in a Greenhouse

The Earth is surrounded by a layer of gases called the atmosphere. The Sun's rays can shine through the atmosphere, but it also keeps in the Sun's heat. When we burn fossil fuels, they release CO_2. CO_2 traps heat so, with more of it in the atmosphere, the Earth is heating up. This is known as **global warming**.

Extreme Weather

As the temperature of the Earth changes, so do our weather patterns. Extreme weather events, such as **drought**, floods, and violent storms, are becoming more common around the world. This is called climate change. Earth's climate varies naturally, but evidence shows that we have made it change more quickly by burning more fossil fuels.

Extreme weather events, such as this hurricane in the United States, are becoming more frequent.

Make Do and Mend

Luckily, there's plenty that each one of us can do to reduce the impact of what we buy on the environment. First, we need to think harder about our shopping habits and see how we can reduce what we buy.

Be a Borrower

We can help to lessen how many new things are made, transported, and sold by not buying new things when we don't really need them. We can borrow or pass on things like toys and clothes to our family and friends, and we can borrow many books, CDs, and DVDs from the library.

We don't keep many of the things we use forever, so it makes sense to borrow them or pass them on.

Make Amends

Have you ever heard of the expression "make do and mend"? During World War II (1939–1945), many resources were used for the war effort, so there were very few things to spare. Women in the UK mended clothes or made "new" ones out of old curtains. Today, many things are thrown away just because they are slightly broken or, even worse, may not be the latest model of something. So see if your toys or clothes can be repaired instead of just throwing them away.

 On June 1, 1941, during World War II, clothes rationing began in the UK. The government put out posters like this one, urging people to make the most of the clothes they already had.

Did you know?

People in the U.S. throw away around 66 pounds (30 kg) of clothes on average every year.

THRIFTY HOME RENOVATION

Did you know that most drills are used for about 15 minutes in their entire lifetime? So, if your parent or carer has a job to do around the house, instead of wasting money on a new drill, why don't you suggest they borrow a neighbor's drill?

Quality, Not Quantity

Sometimes, we do need something that's new, or even just want something that's new. And there's nothing wrong with that, as long as we make wise choices about what we buy.

Will It Last?

Instead of buying lots of things that are cheap, perhaps we should buy fewer things that are well made and will last longer, the way our grandparents used to do. If things last longer, fewer will have to be made, so we put less strain on our environment.

What's It Made Of?

When you do need to buy something, how about doing some "**sustainable** shopping"? If something is sustainable, it means that the materials it's made from are not going to run out. For example, if you buy a wooden desk for your bedroom, look for one that has been "sustainably sourced." This means that the wood used to make the desk has been specially grown to be used, and that new trees will be planted to replace the trees that were cut down.

▲ Some trees, such as pine trees, grow fast and so are a great source of reusable wood.

FSC ©

The Forest Stewardship Council logo shows that wood has been sustainably sourced.

SAVE SOME ENERGY

When your parent or carer is buying a new electrical appliance, such as a washing machine, ask them to look for its energy-efficiency or Energy Star rating to help them choose the most energy-efficient model.

Buying energy-efficient goods can make a big difference to the environment. In just one year, the energy saved in the U.S. by people buying energy-saving goods was the same as taking 25 million cars off the road. That's a lot of energy!

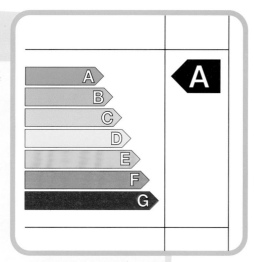

 Energy-efficiency labels like this one from Europe rate goods by their efficiency. "A" is the best.

Throw with Care

If you really don't want something any longer and can't pass it on to someone else, don't just throw it away. Donate it to a Goodwill Shop where it will be sold to raise money for people in need. Or you could ask your parent or carer to help you use a web site such as Freecycle, which can put you in touch with people in your area hoping to find or get rid of all kinds of things. And remember, in the U.S., donations to charity are tax deductible, so your parents can lower their tax bill.

Goodwill Stores sell all kinds of things, from clothes and shoes to books, DVDs, and toys.

Eco Retailers

There are also things that **manufacturers** and retailers can do to help make shopping more friendly to the environment, from cutting down on packaging to running stores on **renewable** energy.

Packaging

Things we buy are packaged to protect them or keep them fresh. However, some packaging is just designed to make the product look attractive, and isn't really necessary. And the more packaging there is that comes with a product, the more there is to throw away.

So, when you can, choose items with less packaging. Remember that the more people choose less heavily packaged goods, the more manufacturers will have to provide them.

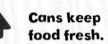 **Cans keep food fresh.**

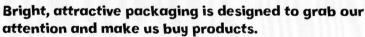 **Bright, attractive packaging is designed to grab our attention and make us buy products.**

Zero Waste

Retailers are already listening to customers who are worried about waste. Walmart, for example, has set itself the goal of having zero-waste stores by 2025—and it owns 4,100 of them! It aims to do this through reducing, reusing, and recycling its products. In particular, Walmart is working with its suppliers to reduce the amount of packaging that comes with its products.

Walmart is leading the way in environmentally friendly shopping.

FOOD POWER!

The British retail chain Marks & Spencer is aiming to make its stores carbon neutral by 2012. This means they won't use up any of the Earth's energy, in the form of fossil fuels, to run their stores. Instead, they plan to use energy from food waste to power their 500 retail outlets in the UK.

Marks & Spencer is well on the way to making its stores carbon neutral.

Buy Recycled!

We can go one step further in environmentally friendly shopping by buying things that have been made from recycled waste. You'd be surprised at some of the things you can buy today!

Recycled into Textiles

When a plastic bottle is recycled, it gets washed, shredded, and melted. It can then be stretched into fibers and woven into thread. It makes a lightweight fabric that can be used to make all sorts of clothes, including T-shirts and fleece jackets.

Just 12 large plastic bottles can be used to produce a warm fleece jacket.

People in the U.S. use 2.5 million plastic bottles every hour, and most of them are thrown away.

What do you mean you're going to be wearing that bottle in a few weeks?

It's All Garbage!

You don't need to stop at clothes! You can buy lots of things made from recycled garbage. "Popsi" claims to be the world's first recycled doll, made from five recycled bottles. And if you're looking for some new garden furniture, why don't you sit on a whole load of plastic bottles? It took about 2,000 plastic bottles to make this colorful picnic table!

There are many things you can buy that are made from recycled garbage, such as this picnic table.

Cycle of Recycling

If we all choose to recycle something we've finished with, that saves a lot from going to landfill. But better still, if we all choose to buy something that is made from recycled materials, and, when we've finished with it, recycle it again, what could be greener than that? We are continuing the cycle of recycling!

Did you know?

In 1960, only 2.8 percent of textiles were reused in the U.S. By 1980, the figure had risen to 6.3 percent and by 2005, 15.3 percent of textiles were reused. Let's keep those figures going up, America!

Responsible Shopping

If you think back to the process of making a T-shirt, there are many different stages involved in making something to sell. And it's important to make sure that at each stage we remember to look after our environment.

A Safe Source

Growing crops such as cotton often involves using chemicals called pesticides, which can pollute our planet. So, some retailers have decided that they will only buy **organic** cotton, which is grown without using these harmful chemicals. Ecolabels tell us which items have been made in the most responsible or environmentally friendly way.

This logo shows that a piece of clothing has been made using cotton that has been produced organically.

CASE STUDY

DON'T WRECK THE RAIN FORESTS

Not only do the Earth's rain forests provide us with food, medicines, and wood, they are also important to keep our environment in balance. Trees "breathe in" the CO_2 we make when we use electricity, drive our cars, and get rid of our waste. By cutting down the rain forests, we risk more CO_2 ending up in the atmosphere and increasing the rate of global warming. So do what you can to protect the rain forest. Visiting the Rainforest Alliance web site (www.rainforest-alliance.org) is a good way to start.

Rain forests absorb CO_2 so they help to keep our atmosphere in balance.

People Power

Using environmentally friendly ways to grow food and make goods isn't the only thing that's important in the whole production process. People are important, too. Many of the things sold in **developed countries** have been made in poorer, **developing countries**.

A Fair Trade

It is important that manufacturers ensure the people who make the products are treated well. You would not think it was OK if you bought a toy cheaply, only to find out it was cheap because it was made by a child who was paid very little and was kept from going to school. Logos or marks by companies such as Fairtrade show when products have been made in a way that looks after the people who made them, as well as the environment.

Did you know?

Fair Trade Certified products are now available at many national restaurants, cafes, and retailers throughout the U.S.

In some countries, children as young as ten work instead of going to school and receiving an education.

Shop, but Remember to Stop!

We live in the most amazing world of natural beauty and seemingly endless resources. But they are not endless. We can all help to protect our planet by changing our shopping habits.

The Three Rs

Have you heard of the three Rs— reduce, reuse, and recycle? Well, we need to do that when we shop. We can reduce the amount we buy by only buying things that we really need, reuse items where we can by borrowing and repairing, and recycle what we no longer need.

We must protect our planet to keep it as beautiful as it is.

Remember to take a reusable bag with you when you go shopping!

MORE EARTHS!

Countries in the developed world, such as those in Europe, and the U.S., use up most of the world's resources. For example, people in the U.S. make up about 5 percent of the world's population, yet put around three times as much pressure on our natural resources than people from the rest of the world. If all the world lived in the same way as the developed world, we would need at least three more Earths just to support the way we live now.

May I please have another Earth?

The Power of You

Don't forget the power of you! If you go to a store and buy a certain type of candy, and all your classmates go into the same store and ask for the same thing, the store will make sure they always keep a supply of those candies to sell. If we all choose to buy products that have come from sustainable sources, are packaged responsibly, and have been made by people who have been treated well, then stores will make sure that is what they sell. That's the power of you. Use it wisely!

How will you use your shopping power?

Glossary

Carbon dioxide A gas in the air around us.

Carbon neutral Not adding any extra carbon dioxide to the atmosphere.

Climate change Long-term changes to the world's weather patterns.

Developed countries Countries with highly developed economies, where most of the population works in factories and businesses.

Developing countries Countries with less developed economies, where most of the population works in farming.

Drought Where there is a shortage of rain over a long period of time.

Energy The power to make or do something.

Environment Surroundings.

Global warming The gradual heating up of the Earth's atmosphere.

Greenhouse gas A gas, such as carbon dioxide, that creates an invisible layer around the Earth, keeping in the heat of the Sun's rays.

Groundwater Water from rain that collects and flows under the Earth's surface.

Harvested Gathered or collected.

Incinerator A giant furnace where waste is burned.

Landfill Areas for dumping and burying household or industrial waste.

Manufacturers Companies that make products.

Materials What something is made from, such as cotton, wood, or metal, for example.

Minerals A substance found in nature.

Natural resources Materials, such as water and wood, that are found in nature.

Organic Produced using environmentally friendly methods, such as not using pesticides.

Pesticides Chemicals used to kill unwanted pests and diseases on plants.

Population The number of people living in a place.

Recycle To break something down so that the materials that it is made from can be used again.

Renewable Something that is in constant supply and will not run out, such as the wind.

Sustainable Able to meet the needs of people now and in the future.

Useful Information

Throughout this book, "real-life measurements" are used for reference. These measurements are not exact, but give a sense of just how much an amount is, or what it looks like.

**Indian elephant =
5 TONS**

**Soccer field = 330 x
230 FEET (100 x 70 M)**

**1 full bathtub =
21 GALLONS (80 L)**

**Olympic-size pool =
660,430 GALLONS
(2,500,000 L)**

Further reading

The Little Green Book of Shopping by Diane Millis (Carlton Books, 2008)

Web Sites

http://www.reuseit.com/
A site selling reusables so you can eliminate disposables from your life.

www.transfairusa.org/
This site keeps you up to date with Fair Trade news and also lists where you can buy Fair Trade certified products throughout the U.S.

www.rainforest-alliance.org/index2.cfm
The education section has stories and projects about the rain forest.

Dates to Remember

Earth Hour—March 28

Earth Day—April 22

World Environment Day—June 5

Clean Air Day—June

Walk to School Campaign—May and October

World Food Day—October 16

America Recycles Day—November 15

Note to parents and teachers: Every effort has been made by the Publishers to ensure that these web sites are suitable for children, that they are of the highest educational value, and that they contain no inappropriate or offensive material. However, because of the nature of the Internet, it is impossible to guarantee that the contents of these sites will not be altered. We strongly advise that Internet access is supervised by a responsible adult.

Index